1

A GLANCE

Twentieth

BY
HENRY HARTSHORNE

"COMING EVENTS CAST THEIR SHADOWS BEFORE."

PHILADELPHIA:
E. CLAXTON & CO.,
930 Market Street.
1881.

[Pg 2]

COLLINS, PRINTER.

[Pg 3]

THE contents of the following pages are taken from a diary, supposed to be written in 1931, by a gentleman of leisure and good opportunities for observation.

Should any reader be inclined to hold the editor or author responsible for what is thus recorded, be it remembered that very little is expressed concerning what *ought* to be; the chief purpose being to show rather what will *probably occur*.

[Pg 4]

[Pg 5]

1931:

A GLANCE AT THE TWENTIETH CENTURY.

January 1, 1931.

I BEGIN to-day to jot down occasional notes of whatever interests me most, in private or public affairs.

Much sympathy is just now felt everywhere for the ex-queen of England in her enforced retirement. She would have been perfectly safe in returning to England; and she will, probably, before long, again take up her residence at Osborne or Balmoral; but the extreme unpopularity of the ex-king makes his return at least undesirable.

[Pg 6]

During our present, 71st Congress, meeting at St. Louis, a motion will be made by a member from Texas for the admission of Mexico as a State. When this is effected, Mexico will be the fifty-second State of our Union. Some Senators are understood to doubt the advantage to the country, at the present time, of this admission, on account of the constitutionally unsettled character of the population. Since Protestantism has so generally prevailed there, however, Mexico is said to have greatly improved. The acceptance of the whole of Central America, in the form of three Territories, must soon follow. For this also, but little can be urged, except the now very old argument of "manifest destiny."

Commercial men say that it is time for this extension to be made, on account of the growing importance of interoceanic navigation, by the three routes, of Panama, Nicaragua, and Tehuantepec. Our large trade with Japan and China requires, besides the steamers running between San Francisco, Yokohama, and Hong Kong every two weeks, more frequent and quick water transit from Philadelphia, New York, Boston, and Baltimore, through one or other of these Isthmian routes.

[Pg 7]

It has been abundantly shown that the anticipation of some speculative persons, that the course of the Gulf Stream, and consequently the climate of Western Europe, might be altered by cutting through the isthmus, and thus connecting the Atlantic and Pacific oceans, was altogether erroneous. No change whatever in the direction, rate of motion, or temperature of the great current has been observed. It is too majestic a movement to be so affected.

It is remarkable how entirely mistaken, also, those croaking prophets were, who formerly supposed that much addition to the old United States would make a cumbrous and impracticable political aggregate. Since the principle that only honest men shall be placed in public offices has been adopted throughout the nation, local administration of local affairs harmonizes so well with a central national government controlling general interests, that all works smoothly yet; even with the addition of the three great States which once formed the Dominion of Canada, and the outlying territories of Greenland, Labrador, Hawaii, Cuba, and St. Domingo.

[Pg 8]

A motion made in the House last year, but then postponed rather than defeated, will probably come up again in Congress at this session: namely, to hold the meeting of Congress every third year in San Francisco. Alternation between Washington and St. Louis has now worked well for eleven years; and Western men are getting clamorous about their right to the same privilege in turn. Capitalists of San Francisco offer to contribute five millions of dollars towards the erection of the western Capitol, besides building and fitting out a Presidential mansion in their city. This is handsome; and, since the central Capitol at St. Louis, now nearly finished, has involved the expenditure of about twelve millions, such liberality may be needful for the success of the project. One of the California Senators has written an article on this topic in the last number of the *North American Review*. He proposes, among other things, that a statue of Abraham Lincoln shall be erected in front of the Capitol at St. Louis, and one of William Penn at that of San Francisco. At the three seats of government we shall then have perpetuated the memory of the three noblest and most era-making of American statesmen: Penn, represent[Pg 9]ing the grandeur and security of Christian justice and

2

peace; Washington, loyalty to national independence and republican institutions; Lincoln, the triumph, by sacrifice, of liberty throughout our continent.

This mention of Abraham Lincoln suggests some retrospection. I remember that when, sixteen years ago, in 1915, our national debt was all finally paid off, great exultation was felt. In a Fourth-of-July oration at Omaha, the speaker, a young colored lawyer, referring to the civil war of 1861-65, as so largely adding to the national debt, said that his grandfather was one of the first men of color who ever sat in the Senate of the United States. Now, there are eight colored Senators, and fifteen members of the House. Of direct African descent also, are the Governor of Louisiana, and the Mayor of the city of Richmond, Virginia; the immediate predecessor of the latter having been a member of one of the oldest historical cavalier families of that State. The general officer in command at West Point, too, is a colored gentleman, of excellent reputation and qualifications. All prejudice of race, in fact, has now very much disappeared,[Pg 10] and is looked back upon as a preposterous error of the past. Indian members of Congress number this session at least seven—two Senators, Cherokees, and five members of the House from the two new States formed from what was once the Indian Territory. The white population of those States is also well represented in the Senate and in the House.

We learn that the United States of South America are at present holding their eighth biennial Congress at Lima, Peru. Brazil continues friendly; but the people of that nation still treasure the traditions and usages of their Empire. The constitutional limitations of Brazil, nevertheless, make it imperial only in name and form; it is as liberal as was the government of Great Britain in the latter days of its monarchy.

We thought it a great deal for the English people, twenty-five years ago, to abolish the place of the House of Lords in their government; or even, before that, so completely to disestablish the once powerful Church of England. But the monarchy! What seemed so permanent as that? Who would have thought, fifty years ago, in good[Pg 11] Queen Victoria's reign, that some persons then living might come to know of her throne being as vacant, nay, as utterly overturned, as the Palace of the Cæsars!

It is one evidence of the old conservatism of the British nation, so terribly shattered now, that the rank, titles, and estates of the nobility are still left to them; with the qualification, that the eldest son is entitled by law to only twice the share of each of the other heirs of the estate; and the whole of any property may be sequestered, by legal process, for debt.

Probably, now, the exodus of British nobles to this country, as well as to the continent of Europe, so active already during the last decade or two, will increase considerably. Marriage of American ladies with lordlings, earls, and even dukes, is scarcely very rare at present; it may be expected soon to become almost as common, at least, as such titles are. It is whispered that it is not entirely impossible that the ex-king and queen, with the royal family, may come hereafter to reside at New Belgravia, in California, where several thousands of acres have been latterly bought and occupied as estates, by English noblemen; or, perhaps[Pg 12] more probably, in Loudon County, Virginia; where the Dukes of Cambridge and of Devonshire both own splendid properties.

No wonder that the Republic of Great Britain and Ireland should differ chiefly from ours, in the greater share of power allotted to the Upper House. If men of rank will (as some of them have already done) wisely accept the inevitable change, and, with full loyalty to the Republic, seek, or allow themselves, to be elected to places in the new Parliament, they may, as Senators, exercise a power and skill in legislation, which will be beneficial not only to their own order, but to their country. They have the advantage of us, in England, in the presidential term being ten years; ours, with difficulty, having been prolonged only to eight. I believe that the preservation of the rank and property of the aristocracy during the critical times just past, and, indeed, the bloodless character of the revolution altogether,—have been mainly due to the sagacious policy of a number of noblemen of large influence;—especially the Argylls in Scotland and the Derbys and Dukes of Northumberland and Bedford, in England, in timely bending[Pg 13] to the storm; yielding, step by step, what *must* be yielded, and so keeping more than if they had resisted all changes to the bitter end.

Especially do they now reap a reward for the good work of the Anglo-Irish Landlords' League; who, with their fitting motto, "*Noblesse oblige*," so liberally purchased from the old landlords, some years since, most of the properties in the distressed and disturbed parts both of England and Ireland, and sold them out in small farms to the peasantry. Glancing the other day, in our library, at Hack Tuke's pamphlet of 1880, on the Distress in Ireland, it is gratifying to know that, to-day, nearly three-fourths of the whole island are possessed by independent peasant farmers.

And India! It reads almost like one of Southey's or Edwin Arnold's oriental poems to peruse the account of the splendid coronation of the Afghan Emperor of All India. Retribution here, indeed, for the folly of that charlatan prime minister who once prated about a "scientific boundary" of the *British* Empire of India. Another instance of the "slow grinding of the mills of the gods," which is so very sure.

[Pg 14]

Good news continues to come from France. Republican principles were never stronger; not a ghost of imperialism, and scarcely a thought of monarchical reaction, appears. Bourbons and Bonapartes alike are politically and sentimentally dead. Evangelical protestantism is spreading and deepening in its influence. The extreme intolerance of Romanism

4

which prevailed for a while is giving way to a more reasonable freedom of conscience for all religions. Yet I doubt whether any city in Europe has fewer Roman Catholic worshippers than Paris, unless it be Rome; where the hatred of all relics and reminders of the old papal days is intense and pervading. It is to be wished that the Italian Republic were as settled and conservative as is that of the French. Spain is now going through its anti-Catholic fever; the banishment of all priests for five years seems an extreme measure; but, after it, there is room for hope that better days than those of Isabella of Castile await this long fallow but once intellectually fertile land. The annexation of Portugal is expected at least as soon as the present king dies; certainly no heir of his will ever wear a crown.

[Pg 15]

The Pope! If he had only read, pondered, and *learned by heart* Victor Hugo's poem, "Le Pape," he might perhaps be still at home in the Vatican. But the "infallible" can never learn. At Constantinople he is at least safe. The Greek government there is secure against all present foes. Then, the triarchate; is it not surprising? Pope, Patriarch, and Primate of Canterbury! Roman, Greek, and Anglican, united at last! A dream of the last century ecclesiastics is fulfilled,—alas, too late; for the glory has departed from the tiara, the crozier, and the mitre altogether.

The Sultan, it is said, has found an asylum in Persia. The Shah allows him a palace, but he is shorn already of half his *hareem*. Perhaps the fate of Lear may be before him yet, though not from filial ingratitude.

[Pg 16]

February 4th, 1931.

IMPORTANT cable news this morning is, that the German republican government last evening passed the bill accepting the proposal of France to purchase Alsace and Lorraine for 300,000,000 francs. More interesting still, a bill was also introduced, and is likely to pass, *ceding* to the French all the rest of the territory on the west side of the Rhine bordering on France. The long-coveted natural boundary will thus be theirs. How infinitely better this than war upon war for revenge and conquest!

The tunnel under the British Channel is nearly finished. It is to be constantly illuminated with electric light, and, being a joint national work, will be a free public (not *high*way exactly, but) way, for all.

Austria-Hungary appears to be, for a time at least, tranquil. The emperor has conceded all that the constitutionalists required of him. There are now only four emperors in the world:—those of Austria, Brazil, India, and China; and the first[Pg 17] two are so limited in power as hardly to deserve the imperial name. The title of tsar has been definitely denied to the present constitutional monarch of Russia; he is really something between a king and a president.

Fearful indeed must have been the communist or nihilist war of Russia of thirty years ago. The country has hardly recovered from it yet.

5

Had it not been for the loyalty of the large population of those families emancipated in 1861 by the Tsar Alexander II. from serfdom, not only the imperial family, but all the members of the nobility, and the whole class of wealthy Russians would probably have been put to death by fire and sword.

Welcome to all lovers of peace and prosperity will be the late intelligence that, at the Congress of Berlin, all the great powers have agreed to reduce their standing armies to 50,000 men for each nation; and that neither power shall increase its forces, without two months' notice to all the rest. The "volunteer" military organizations will still be allowed, besides these armies; but zeal for rifle practice seems to be very much on the wane. It is probable that occasional showy parades may[Pg 18] soon be all that is left in civilized countries of the "pomp and circumstance of glorious war."

It is painful to know that in Africa, and in Mongolian Asia, the arts of destruction have been more rapidly borrowed from Europe than those of peace and progress. It is said that Gatling guns, as well as Minié rifles and dynamite shells, and the newly reinvented projectile Greek fire, are now in use with terrible effect between hostile tribes in Central Africa, officered in great part by European and American adventurers.

The international coinage arrangement, on the decimal system, so long in use between England, France, Germany, Italy, and the United States, will be extended next year, by agreement, to Spain, Russia, Denmark, and Greece. It is wonderful how our fathers, even almost down to the present generation, were satisfied with any scheme of weights and measures other than the metrical, now so universally in use.

From the South African Dutch-English Federal States we hear of settlement and progress. The Australian Republic also is thriving. Melbourne[Pg 19] has now 600,000 inhabitants. How many millions of people to-day speak the English language! All North America (except a part of the people of Mexico); Australia; India; South Africa; and, this month, after long consideration, Japan has officially adopted English as the language of public affairs, to be taught in all the common schools. By the way, the newly elected Secretary of Education of the Japanese Commonwealth is an American; a graduate of the High School at Chicago. The extension of the use of spoken, written, and printed English in China is quite rapid, and so it is in Egypt, on the Continent of Europe, and in South America. It truly bids fair within a century to become the universal language.

The purchase of Jerusalem and the greater part of Palestine by an association of wealthy Jews, headed by the Rothschild, Montefiore, and Belmont families, is an accomplished fact. Along with this it may be noted that very many Jews have recently been converted to Christianity. There is a large tabernacle for the worship of evangelical Jews just built upon the

Mount of Olives. At one of the first meetings of the San[Pg 20]hedrim after the Russian municipal government had been withdrawn, a rabbi, bearing the significant name of Nicodemus, proposed this question for discussion: "Ought we now to acknowledge Jesus as the Messiah?" By a small majority, the question was indefinitely postponed without debate.

Jerusalem is now lit by gas, except an electric light in one of the central streets. Horse-cars are running in every direction; and a steam-train passes daily to and from Jaffa on the Mediterranean. The Mosque of Omar has been purchased by the Young Men's Christian Association, which has within its walk a Bible-School of nearly 1000 pupils of all ages. A college for both sexes is in full operation at Jericho. An English weekly and an American daily newspaper are issued in Jerusalem, and an English daily paper also in Smyrna.

We learn that the Joint Commission appointed by England, France, Italy, and Greece for the provisional government of Egypt, is meeting with fair success; bad as the financial state of that country has been. The American "Egyptian Improvement Company," with a capital of forty millions of dollars, is paying an annual dividend of six per[Pg 21] cent.; which is extraordinary for these times. New explorations along the Nile, near Luxor, have unearthed a number of royal tombs, with extremely interesting paintings, sarcophagi, and hieroglyphic inscriptions. More notable still; in a Coptic convent in Upper Egypt, there has been found a Greek Codex of the whole New Testament; believed by palæographers to belong to the third century. Among other things, it omits the concluding verses of the last chapter of the Gospel of Mark, and attaches the name of Barnabas to the Epistle to the Hebrews; not containing, moreover, the reputed Epistle of Barnabas which was found attached to the Sinaitic Codex.

[Pg 22]
March 26th, '31.

A telegram directly from Peking to Washington announces the extension to all the provinces in China of the decree, already for a number of years enforced in the great cities, totally prohibiting the sale of opium; except by a few government appointees, at prescription of registered physicians.

The Euphrates Valley Railroad is almost finished. The main line of communication between Europe and Asia will pass through Smyrna, Aleppo, Bagdad, and Bassora on the Persian Gulf. A road will also run from Jaffa through Jerusalem, and will connect with Damascus. Parlor, sleeping, and hotel cars will be placed on all these roads at once, furnished by an Indianapolis firm on contract.

By the completion, many years ago, of the trans-Indian line of telegraph and railroad, and now of that from Calcutta along the Brahmapootra River and through Southern China to Canton, the girdle around the world is almost completed. Puck might travel it now in less than forty minutes.[Pg 23] Behring's Strait will, in a few months, be crossed by the Asian-American cable, and a line of steamers, owned partly by Russian and partly by American stockholders, will soon make that channel a ferry between the Continents. The greatest tunnel in the world is that being constructed through a spur of the Himalayas, in Northeastern India. The new observatory on Mount Everest is furnished with three first-class telescopes, and other needful appliances for astronomical observation.

All friends of Africa will rejoice to know that Liberia is extending its annexations farther and farther into the interior. The Livingstone lock Canal also, along the valley of what was once called the Congo River, is contracted for, to be ready for navigation within twelve months. No doubt at all exists of the success of the project for irrigating portions of the desert of Sahara by means of Artesian, or rather not very deep driven wells, by which the desert has already been made, in a hundred artificial oases, to "blossom as the rose."

Ship canals seem to be among the special works[Pg 24] of our time. It is now almost a quarter of a century since the Caspian and Black Seas were connected, through the enterprise of Russian capitalists. The newest project broached is to cut through from the Gulf of Boothia to Hudson's Bay, in latitude 65° N. and longitude 90° W. from Greenwich.

I think I shall join, this summer, one of the excursions which are getting so fashionable, to Labrador, Greenland, or perhaps Iceland. The Upernavik House is said to be very well kept, and filled most of the season with boarders or transient visitors.

There is something yet new in these northern places. Switzerland is getting spoiled and commonplace. Think of making the ascent of Mont Blanc on a steam railroad! Think, too, of public school excursions to the Yosemite, and the rocks there being placarded all over (until the government very properly had them taken down) with advertisements!

Certainly man must begin to repair or restore to nature some of his robberies. A small begin[Pg 25]ning of this has been made by the Society of Acclimatization and Conservation. At their Acclimatarium in West Philadelphia, including the old Centennial Grounds of '76, and the Zoological Garden, munificent arrangements have been made, by the use of glass, wood, iron, and water-gas heating apparatus, for the creation of an artificial tropical and sub-tropical climate. All the glories of Southern India, Ceylon, Java, Australasia, Brazil, and the West Indies may now be seen there, in palms, cycads, eucalypti, acacias, tree ferns, clinging vines, and splendid flowers, as well as in the many-colored birds and insects of those regions; with their animals, also, which are disposed, when needful for safety, in cages so large and yet so light, as scarcely to give the appearance of imprisonment.

8

Also, the camel is now fairly naturalized in Texas and New Mexico, and the two-toed ostrich in South America; on the pampas of that continent travellers may meet with the gazelle, the springbok, the oryx, and the kangaroo. Elephants are domesticated and used for court occasions in Brazil, as they are in India. Tea and coffee are now largely cultivated in California, Georgia, Ten[Pg 26]nessee, North Carolina, and Virginia. In exchange, the cinchona tree abounds more now in India than in Peru, and the cacao or cocoa tree has been planted by thousands upon the southern slopes of the Himalayas and in Persia.

On the other hand, the bison and the prong-buck are almost extinct in the west. But for the great national parks, Yellowstone, Yosemite, Niagara and others, carefully guarded, the American deer, elk, and moose would all likewise disappear. Forest-culture, however, is, by the pressure of necessity, attracting, as it ought, a great deal of attention, under the guidance of the government Agricultural Department.

It seems to work well, better than some expected, to have our national Cabinet enlarged by the introduction to full rank in it of the three new Secretaries, of Agriculture, Education, and Health. The importance of the last named of these is universally acknowledged; as well as the necessity for State Boards of Health in all the States.

How much sanitation has advanced during the last half century! Human life now averages 50[Pg 27]years in the United States; rather more in England, and nearly as much in France and Germany. By stringent regulations for maintaining cleanliness of ships, wharves, and, indeed of cities throughout, along with the abolition everywhere of the useless and detestable antiquated personal quarantine, yellow fever has been almost absolutely extinguished; only ten deaths from it occurring last summer in Havana, one or two in Pensacola, and not one in New Orleans, Memphis, Nashville, or any other city in the United States. Cholera, likewise, through sanitary improvements, has disappeared from the world, except a score or two of cases annually in the worst crowded villages near the Ganges in India. What a grand triumph of medical art, also, following Jenner's vaccination, and Pasteur's later investigations, is the protection afforded against the dangers of scarlet fever, measles and whooping-cough, by inoculation with a modified virus, appropriate to each!

But, more than these, the waste of human life has been abridged by the sweeping reform effected in regard to the abuse of alcohol. That was a grand report made to Congress by the men and women of the "Alcohol Commission" of 1910.[Pg 28] It is said to have been principally written by the chairwoman of the Commission, who was then, and continues to be still, Professor of Political Economy in Harvard University. Local option in nine-tenths of our States, with prohibition of dram-shops everywhere: what a change from a century ago! A man was almost mobbed in Boston the other day for selling liquor to a minor. On being taken before a magistrate, and afterwards tried in court, he was imprisoned for three years. Arrests, fines and imprisonment for selling whiskey by the glass, rather frequent ten years ago in New York, are seldom now heard of. The American people are sober! It looks like a monstrous and incredible folly that we read of, that, once, even otherwise sensible and well-meaning gentlemen would, on occasion, get staggering drunk.

Wines of the finest quality, equal to the best of Europe, are made every year in California, New York, and Missouri; and they are occasionally placed upon the table at entertainments. But it is regarded as an intolerable indecorum for a gentleman to drink more than a single glass, or a lady half a glass, at a time.

There is no doubt that the large and magnificent[Pg 29] coffee and cocoa houses (the latter most commended on hygienic grounds), in all our great cities, have made much more practicable the shutting up of the drinking saloons that formerly lined our streets.

Another great sanitary improvement was the destruction, a few years since, of all the tenement houses of New York and Boston, and the prohibition by law of their re-erection. The mortality of New York was lessened by one-third the very next year after it was done. I am glad to hear that, following this good example, a Citizens' Philanthropic Building Association has bought up most of the ground in the worst parts of the down town Philadelphia suburbs, in order to put up blocks of model lodging-houses there. It seems unfortunate that the terribly destructive fire in Philadelphia in 1890, occurring when all the fireplugs were frozen with zero weather, should have laid waste Arch, Market, Chestnut, and Walnut Streets, rather than those dens of poverty and misery.

When the new water supply for New York city[Pg 30] and the Hudson River towns from the Adirondack region, and those for Philadelphia from the upper Delaware and Perkiomen, are completed, and sewage irrigation relieves the rivers everywhere from pollution, it may be hoped that the yearly mortality of our great communities may be brought down below 15 in 1000; once thought to be the acme of healthfulness.

Cheapening of food goes on remarkably, along with close and high culture of the ground. Proper appreciation of the share taken by the *atmosphere* in the nutrition of plants has made soil construction a much simpler and surer thing than formerly. Roof-gardens in towns are very common and successful; half of the vegetables consumed in Baltimore are said to be grown on roofs. I once saw a book entitled "Our Farm of Four Acres;" and another, "Ten Acres Enough." Very little skill should be needed now to enable a frugal family to live *well* on two or three acres of well-made ground.[Pg 31]

August 20th, 1931.

I bought yesterday a pound of the best grass-flavored adipo-butyrin (as good as any dairy butter) for ten cents; a sirloin of good western beef for twelve cents a pound; and, best of all, a bushel of Rocky-mountain grasshoppers, as crisp and delicious as could be, for only thirty-seven cents! They say, the supply of these last delicacies will be short this season; as hardly any have appeared yet in Kansas or Nebraska. Excursions for procuring them from farther west are, however, quite frequently made.

I saw an account of the sale of some Southern lands in this morning's paper. The best farm land in Virginia brings 400 to 500 dollars an acre. Some in South Carolina has brought 400 and 500; good Maryland farms 5, 6, and 700 dollars an acre. Manufactories, too, are in active operation in all the old Cotton States. It has happened, as every one might have known would be the case, that when a generation or two had passed after the[Pg 32] cessation of slavery, and the old hatreds had been buried in the graves of the men and women who nursed them, prosperity would increase in the South to an extent that could hardly be imagined under the slaveholding régime, the "dark ages" of America.

How fast arts and inventions are accumulating! The nineteenth century seems likely to be equaled if not surpassed in new material appliances of civilization and luxury. Railroad speed now often reaches ninety miles an hour, upon the straightened and generally elevated tracks in use; with the automatic block-signal system so complete, that collisions are nearly impossible. Coal-oil is now much used in locomotives, and almost universally on ocean steamers. The supposed dangers of its conveyance and employment have been readily met by suitable precautions.

The cable-telephone has been perfected; one can converse directly with a friend or business correspondent in Liverpool, London, or Paris, at the rate of twelve cents a minute. How these things promote terseness and pithiness of speech! I believe no one, unless it be the stockholders of[Pg 33]one or two old lines, regrets that all telegraphic and telephonic communication in this country has been taken under the control of the government. Underground laying of telegraph wires is now nearly universal.

Photographing in colors, a French invention, is one of the newer and more attractive arts. Printing one's own books has become almost too easy, by using the type-writer, with sheets of celluloid, warmed to 300°, instead of paper. The celluloid hardens at once sufficiently for stereotyping; so that any number of thousands of copies can be taken from such off-hand plates. Truly, "of making many books there is no end." Pencils, moreover, whose marks are permanent, have so improved as to render that intolerably nasty fluid, ink, unnecessary, and confined in its use entirely to a few old-fashioned people.

Magnifying sound has gone far beyond the microphone and megaphone of the last century. Deaf persons are now helped by instrumental aid almost as much as defective sight is by proper glasses.

Gunpowder and nitro-glycerin have both been utilized for the production of continuous motion,[Pg 34] especially in the propulsion of the contents of transportation tubes. By these agencies, all the local letter distribution of Boston and Portland, and a good deal of that of New York, is effected by tube-transmission to and from the various branch deposit-offices of the cities.

Locomotives are at present running, at a speed limited by law, on our best common roads. Several wealthy gentlemen in Philadelphia use small private steam-carriages to go daily between their homes and places of business. The *pocket magneto-electric lamp* is one of the neatest of modern inventions; and *wiring power* one of the most tremendous. It is said that the energy of a twenty-horse-power steam engine may be conveyed from place to place as far as 25 or 30 miles, by suitable cable under ground. The only difficulty is to make its management safe, as the least contact with the cable is as destructive as lightning; but this will no doubt soon be done.

With all these ingenuities, no one has yet contrived a really successful flying-machine. Man seems designed by his Creator to remain always "a little lower than the angels" in this prerogative.

It is a good thing to be able to be rid, as we[Pg 35] now may be, of dirty anthracite or other coal in our houses. The distribution of heat,—by pipes conveying hydrogen gas for burning in gas-stoves, ranges, or furnaces, by steam, or by hot water,—is provided for on the pipe system, extending under and through houses from large street mains, in most of our cities. I am much pleased also with the method of *floor* and *wall-*warming now common; although, for the wealthy, an open wood fire is still one of the greatest of all costly luxuries. The uses of coal, moreover, are yet so numerous, that all coal-carrying railroads are earning and paying large dividends.

For the summer time, the "can't get away" Philadelphians may be congratulated on the delightful sea-water baths they can have on Broad Street, in water brought by the great marine aqueduct from Atlantic City. The water is raised from the sea by tidal power (a kind of motor now having many applications) to a reservoir at a sufficient height to give the requisite descent towards the city. Its rate of movement, also, is such that, being under cover all the way, it retains much of the coolness of the ocean-surf.

The blanching or bleaching of the London fogs,[Pg 36] by the improved methods of consuming smoke, must be a very fine thing for the dwellers in that overgrown city. We hear, however, of one old lady, a duchess, who thinks the fog now to be very vulgarly pale; and regrets the good old days of what she thought a much more picturesque gloom.

[Pg 37]
October 3d, 1931.

12

I have just walked up from the Public Buildings at Broad and Market Streets, whither I went to read the "City Bulletin" of telegraphic intelligence from all quarters of the world. This is displayed by means of letters thrown by the electric light upon screens on the four sides of the great square tower above the public buildings. On the North side, you can see the latest items of news from Europe; on the East, from Asia; on the South, from South America, Africa, and Australasia; on the West, from all parts of the United States and Territories. The illumination is kept up until 10 o'clock every night.

Of items thrown out this evening, I remember only these: from Europe, that the Pan-Catholic Council of the three historical churches (so called), has decided to admit the precedence, but not the supremacy, of the Pope over the Patriarch of the Greek Church and the Anglican Primate. Between the latter two, the question of relative rank has not yet been decided. From Asia, report comes[Pg 38] of a terrible battle between the Persians and the invading Tartar army, in which the latter was defeated, with great loss on both sides. All the European and American ambassadors are instructed to urge the conclusion of this useless but ferocious war. From Africa, we are told of the election of a new President, of Dutch descent, for the South African Federation. Of United States intelligence of to-day, I am most interested to learn that the intercollegiate prize for oratory, at Washington, for which the students of twenty-five colleges competed, has been awarded to Miss Minnie Stephens, a young lady of Atlanta, Georgia.

The International Weather Signal Service now covers, in its communications, all portions of the globe. Predictions, or at least indications, for three days ahead, are posted daily at Washington (whence they are sent to our other American cities), and at London, Berlin, St. Petersburg, Constantinople, Bombay, Calcutta, Canton, Tokio, Cairo, Cape Town, Sydney, Rio Janeiro, Lima, Havana, and Vera Cruz.

What a practical comment upon the uselessness of our petty standing regular army of twenty-five[Pg 39] thousand men is the act of Congress just passed, making West Point a school for Signal Service officers, and for training those preparing for Arctic, Antarctic, and Ocean-dredging explorations!

Speaking of institutions of education, the National University has completed its endowment of six million dollars, and has commenced its organization by the appointment of a Board of Directors. It is to be located at Chicago, St. Louis, or Omaha, as the Board shall conclude. For the President of this University, an evening paper rather lightly says: "so much difficulty exists in selecting an individual belonging to this world, combining all the desired requisites, that it is in contemplation to wait (our moon being uninhabited) until one can be obtained from the planet Mars, or possibly Jupiter. The latter will no doubt be best,—as one who can bear the great heat of that planet will be well fitted to meet the fiery criticism to which he will be subjected on all sides."

Industrial and half-time manual-labor schools are now, in the public school systems of our States, getting to be the rule rather than the exception. Astonishing it is, also, to look back to the time, which I can remember, when, instead of the natu[Pg 40]ral and rational method of coeducation of the sexes, now universal (with very few exceptions), it was a common thing for boys and girls, young men and young women, to be educated,—monastery and nunnery fashion,—entirely apart!

Out-of-door schools are a grand improvement of our times. They are the old kindergartens of Pestalozzi and Froebel developed. The best that I know is in West Philadelphia, near the Acclimatarium. In winter, the teachers and children go together for study into the inclosures of the Acclimatarium, for at least three hours every day. In summer, their range is extended through Fairmount Park, and farther, for the same or a longer period. The pupils enter this school at six or seven years of age, and continue the "nature course" until twelve or thirteen. Then they take up, elsewhere, a larger share of book studies; so that they may be, by sixteen, seventeen, or eighteen, prepared for college, if desired; and after college, for the Universities.

The degrees of Bachelor and Master of Education, first bestowed by some of the great Western Universities, are now granted also by most of our kindred Eastern institutions.[Pg 41]

Everybody is satisfied that the great English Spelling Reform is not going on too fast. Our children are taught the new spelling, the books being, in all the public schools, changed once in ten years. With this gradual transition, under the direction of the Anglo-American Philological Association, we are safely approaching an era of reasonable orthography.

A seemingly extreme rule, but really very good, has lately been passed by the directors of three of the largest public libraries in this country, at the urgency of the Department of Mental Hygiene of the American Social Science Association. It is, that no novels shall be given out on the application of minors; and that only one novel in three months may be taken out in any one stockholder's name.[Pg 42]

December 1st, 1931.

The presidential address at the annual meeting of the Intercontinental Scientific Congress, this year held at Melbourne, Australia, has just been published. I find in it mention of the following, among other, late advances in science.

Proof seems to be accumulating that the suggestion made by Lockyer in 1879, that all the supposed chemical elements are really modifications of the same substance, and that soon after made by others, that this common substance is only *condensed universal ether*, the medium of luminous, electrical, and other vibrations, is going to be accepted as correct. The opinion that the *panæther*, as it is best called, is *not atomic* in its constitution, while all the combinable elements are so, is also gaining ground.

More exact knowledge being now had of the relations existing among the different so-called elements, it has become possible to work out the atomic theory, so far as to prove that the law of chemical attraction is identical with that of gravi[Pg 43]tation; namely, that its force is directly in proportion to the number and mass of the atoms, and inversely as the squares of their distances:*atomic distances* being, by extremely abstruse calculations, approximately estimated. The long wished for full explanation of the relations between frictional electricity, voltaism, magnetism, heat, and light, seems likely soon to be obtained; and, consequently, also the exact physical relations of the vital or formative force of animals and plants.

It is quite well understood that, as Newton himself anticipated, the law of gravitation was but a step, though a very great and important one, in the generalization of cosmic changes and forces. We seem to be on the eve of another advance, needing only the completion of some difficult mathematical and physical analyses,—in which all so-called attractions and repulsions whatever will be resolved into results or phenomena of motion; ethereal, atomic, molecular, and massive motions; whose mutual reactions and momenta make the infinite complexity of the universe. Towards such a conclusion, serviceable contributions were made many years since, by three American cosmologists, Norton, Pliny Chase, and Kirkwood.

[Pg 44]
The 320th asteroid was discovered at Pike's Peak observatory, during last summer. I may jot down here too, the record of the first observation of a new telescopic comet, last month, by a senior student of Bryn Mawr College for Women.

Australia, according to the address mentioned, has at last furnished to palæontologists the real *missing link*, not between men and apes, which they have generally given up, but between vertebrate and invertebrate animals. So that the famous ascidian mollusc, with a semi-vertebral larval stage, which nourished in the writings of Darwin and others, is no longer needful. The fossil referred to is an ancient fish-like worm, or worm-like fish, to which the name of Entomicthys amphisoma has been provisionally given. It is still more remarkable than the amphioxus or lancelet, which has been long known.

By the improved methods of measuring both space and time in practical astronomy, it has been rendered nearly or quite certain that our earth is gradually approaching the sun; and that the same is true of all the other planets. Small as the rate of this approach is, it is enough to confirm the belief of Sir William Thomson and others in the[Pg 45] 19th century, that our solar system is constructed for finite (not, as Laplace and

Lagrange thought, infinite) duration; the whole economy of planets will at last run down like a clock, and all the elements will be melted together with fervent heat.

Among the leading discoveries of the year is that of the long-looked-for third moon of the extra-Neptunian planet. The name of that planet itself, although it has been known since 1885, is not yet finally settled. Some call it Pluto; others Terminus; it being almost certainly the outermost body of our solar system.

A good observation of the intra-Mercurial planet Vulcan was made from Mount Everest some weeks ago, by the Hindu astronomer-imperial on duty there.

Of the *corona* seen around the sun during eclipses, the tendency now seems to be to return to the explanation long ago proposed and discarded; that it is neither telluric, *i.e.* produced by our atmosphere, nor, strictly or only, solar; but mainly *selenic*; that is, caused by the rays of the sun being *diffracted* around the edge of the moon intervening between us and it. The different appearances of the corona as seen from different[Pg 46] places on the earth are thus accounted for, as well as their diversity during different eclipses, by the irregularities upon the lunar surface.

A fine chemical advance has been made in the laboratory of the University of Vienna, in the manufacture, from strictly *inorganic* materials, and at very moderate and remunerative cost, of the alkaloids quinia, strychnia, atropia, morphia, and others. No chemist, however, has yet made a single speck of albumen, or any other truly protoplasmic substance. By the consent of all biologists, the disproof of the possibility of "spontaneous generation" is as strong as ever.

How utterly impossible is it for any one to keep up with the science or the literature of the present day! One must have the hundred hands of Briareus, and the hundred eyes of Argus, with brains to suit, to know anything at all worth while, in our age. Happily, it is not expected of us, of anybody, to be Aristotles or Humboldts now.

I like very much the Philadelphia Library Public Reading Course, carried on for the last seven or eight years. The Readers there give, twice every week, summary oral accounts of all that has[Pg 47] been last printed in all parts of the world; one hour each evening being given to literature, and another hour to science. Once a month, the latest important books are briefly reviewed. This saves busy people a vast deal of time. The Reader is a sort of animated newspaper and monthly magazine combined.

In social life, the once neglected accomplishment and enjoyment of conversation are coming up again. The "Conversation Club" is a great success. Its members meet once a week, ladies and gentlemen, young and old, single and married, together, at each other's houses, to the number of from fifty to a hundred and fifty; from half past seven or eight, to half past ten sharp, without any of the trouble or expense of food or drink;

which it is rationally supposed they have all had or can get at home. Dancing is omitted, and only vocal music is allowed; this being in rooms apart from the main parlors. With those living out of town, afternoon hours are preferred; and only tea, coffee, cocoa, and crackers are placed on side tables for those who come from distant places. Similar *salons* to these are usual in Paris; one of them occurring on the same evening in the week as ours.[Pg 48] Last week, by arrangement, a half hour's telephonic discussion was maintained between Philadelphia and Paris, on the merits of the last two French translations of Longfellow's Poems.

Twice at least in the winter there are yet larger gatherings of the same kind, at our Academy of Natural Sciences, and at the Academy of Fine Arts. In these, 500 or 600 people are commonly assembled; and very pleasant occasions they always are.

The "new Raphael" is the name rather oddly given to a young painter of extraordinary genius, especially for depicting the human face and form. Oddly given, I say, because the artist is a young woman, daughter of a respected minister of the Society of Friends, living in North Carolina.

A Greek poet, chiefly lyric, recalling Pindaric days, has sprung up lately in Athens. His rendering of the dramas of Sophocles into modern Greek for the stage in Athens and Constantinople, is said to have attracted much attention amongst theatre-goers.

A reunion of literary men and women of all nations is to be held at Athens, in view of the ruins of the Parthenon, during May, next year.

A trial is now going on in this city, which is[Pg 49] likely to illustrate well the difference between the present method of trial by courts of judges, and the old way by juries. Three judges must always be present; and the statement of the accused, in criminal cases, is taken as part of the evidence. The abomination of allowing lawyers to engage *expert* witnesses on behalf of their respective sides, on questions of poisoning or insanity, has been done away with. The court, in such cases, appoints a commission of experts, who make a joint report in every instance.

Capital punishment has been abolished in all our States, and in all European countries except Spain, Portugal, and Russia. Life-imprisonment has taken its place; without pardoning power anywhere, even when the plea of insanity has been sustained. A great gain in our jurisprudence latterly is, making the proved *intent and effort to kill* identical before the law with successful murder. Moreover, repeated crimes, burglaries for instance, are punished by cumulative increase of the penalty after every new offence and conviction. As all imprisonment is now conducted on the separate plan, jails are no longer, as once, training schools for crime.

[Pg 50]
December 25th, 1931.

17

The bells are ringing for the various church celebrations of Christmas. I will, as I hear them, jot down some items about late religious affairs. In yesterday's "Anglo-American Weekly Times," I read a well-written sermon by the Dean of St. Paul's, London, on the evidence of the wisdom and goodness of God derived from the facts of evolution; not Darwinism, as that phase of the theory of development has latterly become practically of secondary importance. Justice was done, however, in this discourse, to the immense contributions made by Darwin's genius and labors to the facts of natural science, and to the proofs of design abounding in the creation.

The revised version of the Bible (of which the New Testament was issued in 1881) is now universally in use. The version of King James, so called, has become antiquated, and is consulted almost alone by scholars for special inquiries. Editions are now to be had of the later version in which the reformed spelling of 1925 is carried out.

[Pg 51]

The Old Catholics, of whom Döllinger and Loyson (Father Hyacinthe) were leaders during the last century, have carried their reforms much farther than the High Church section of the Anglican body. They are, it is said, looking towards junction with the Reformed Episcopal Church, which now numbers about 600,000 members.

A striking feature in the religious "movement" of our times, is a general tendency towards the *congregational* principle of association. Councils, convocations, synods, conventions, and "yearly meetings" have more and more an advisory, and less and less of compulsory power, over independent local congregations. Denominations have so multiplied, that it looks as if, after awhile, every man may be his own pastor, elder, bishop, or over-seer,—indeed a whole "church" by himself. Let us hope that this disintegration only anticipates the final *reunion* of all Christians in one flock (perhaps even in one fold), under one shepherd.

The World's Young Men's Christian Association now counts more than two million members. Its annual conventions meet alternately at Philadelphia, San Francisco, New Orleans, Washington, London, Rome, Constantinople, Jerusalem, Cal[Pg 52]cutta, Melbourne, and Tokio. Women's Christian Associations number, in the aggregate, almost as many members.

On New Year's day, 1932, a union prayer meeting of all nations is to convene under the dome of St. Peter's at Rome. It will be continued daily for two weeks. At least ten languages will be used by those there assembled for united worship.

At the Pan-Presbyterian Convention, met at San Francisco on the 15th of last month, a resolution was passed, after protracted debate, in which it was declared to be the sense of that body that Christian doctrine, in the progress of modern enlightenment, must not be hereafter fettered

18

by any prescription, however venerable, of merely human authority; no minister being bound, therefore, to exclusive adherence, in his statement of doctrines, to language not contained in the Holy Scriptures. This was understood as allowing, as entirely optional, the abandonment of what has been known as predestinarian Calvinism.

Three weeks later, in the Unitarian Convention at Boston, the following resolution was brought forward:

[Pg 53]—

"Whereas, the occasion for the origin of New England Unitarianism was the need of protesting against extreme and erroneous dogmatic teaching, whereby the truth and beauty of Christianity were becoming obscured and misrepresented; and whereas, at the present day, reform in this respect has become general among the so-called Evangelical churches:

"Therefore Resolved, that the mission of Unitarianism in this country may be regarded as having been performed and ended."

This was passed by a fair majority. The dissenters, after the adjournment of the Convention, reorganized on the same basis as before, with a view to permanence; but several of these joined, somewhat later, the Association of Free Religionists, who have discarded the name of Christians.

A Congress of German philosophers and advocates of free thought was held some months ago at Munich. At its closing session, a declaration was proposed as embodying the main present result of free thought in Germany. It sets forth that the ideas of Christianity are necessary to a satisfactory theory of man and the universe. These ideas are[Pg 54] said to be, the existence and eternity of God, the visible manifestation of God to man, the suffering of God with and for man, and the visitation of God, spiritually, to men.

The facts of physical and natural science, interpreted according to the matured scheme of evolution, prove a *beginning*, a world not eternal. The philosophy of the Absolute requires recognition of the existence of an *unbeginning* and unending Being. Cosmic science proves *unity of plan, purpose*, and *beneficence*, throughout the universe. Man's intelligence necessitates the belief that a greater Intelligence must have created him. If, then, God is, and is good, it is impossible that He should not make Himself known to man, both visibly and invisibly: once, at least, in history, and always spiritually. If man, being free, errs, he must, by the necessity of the laws of the universe, in deranging its harmony, suffer and cause suffering. But God may Himself accept this suffering, and so abate it; making it finite and brief, instead of unending, as it must, without His interference, be. All these conditions are met by the Christian religion; which has also stood the severe test of many martyrdoms. "While, therefore,"[Pg 55] it is concluded, "we regard ecclesiasticism and ritualism as among the greatest of evils, we are convinced that Christianity is the only religion reconcilable with philosophy; and we therefore accept it as true."

This declaration is reported to have met with very loud and angry dissent from a considerable minority. The latter resolved themselves, finally, into two schools: one, the larger in number, of rational deists or theists, repudiating Christianity; the more extreme portion, into a new sect or organization, which met shortly afterwards in Dresden.

These last free-thinkers, when assembled, declared that they were discontented with all previous protests against religion, as not going sufficiently far. "We have had enough," they said, "of futile efforts to deny or ignore the existence of God. We believe that He exists, and we *hate*Him. We regard the Satan of Milton as the noblest character in all literature and history. All honor from us to those who, in history like Strauss, in philosophy like Schopenhauer, in science like Hœckel, and in literature like Heine, have tried, directly or indirectly, to make the Christian's God seem unknowable or hateful to men. But the time has[Pg 56] come to pass beyond their moderation. We unite ourselves in a league, not as atheists, but as *misotheists*, against all that is called God; not in unbelief, but in revolt and utter defiance."

Such is the substance of the programme, announced on the pages of the "Anarchist," published in New York, of the new Misotheistic Association. It fraternizes, very naturally, with the Anti-Christian Society of London, and the Grand Order of the Knights of Lucifer at Rome.

Lower down in the scale still, but with much the same *animus*, is the secret order, now said to number many members in nearly every city in Europe and this country, though originating in Bombay, India, of *Thugs* and *Burners*. These are vowed to take every opportunity to do injury to the cause not only of religion, but of public and private virtue and order; by arson, assassination, and other crimes. Through the vigilance of well-organized police, they have, so far, been prevented from effecting very much mischief; but they constitute one of the worst of all the dangers of our otherwise generally secure civilization.

In the Calcutta "Weekly Record of Asia," just arrived, I find particulars of the late conversion of[Pg 57] the young Emperor of China to Christianity, and of the consequences of that event.

His instructor, a few years ago, while teaching him the English language, selected the Bible as the best specimen of its literature. Reading it alone, he became interested in it, and at last convinced of its truth. When a Moravian missionary requested and obtained an interview with him, his faith was confirmed. As soon as he came to the throne, he resolved, after much prayer, fully to act out his new belief. Confiding this state of mind to one of his trusted counsellors, such changes were made in his household and government as would insure the prompt and effective carrying out of the imperial mandates. Then he caused a proclamation to be made throughout the empire, that he, the Emperor, acknowledged the God of the Christians' Bible, and commanded all his faithful children to accept the religion of Christ. So much had been done already by persevering mission-work in China, as well as in India, that the people were not altogether unprepared for this change.

But more was to come yet. In the solitude of his chamber, the Emperor became satisfied that the God of Christianity is a God of Peace. War[Pg 58] must be absolutely forbidden and brought to an end. In a second proclamation, all his subjects were commanded to lay down their arms; and disarmament began at the imperial palace itself; maces alone being thenceforth carried by its officers and guards.

At this juncture, a rebellion occurred, headed by a descendant of the leader of the great rebellion of the nineteenth century. A considerable undisciplined army of disaffected men was brought together, and they marched toward Peking. The Emperor summoned his grand mandarins, and also his chief religious advisers, two venerable native Christian men. Between these, he was borne out in his palanquin upon the great highway, followed by the imperial guard, unarmed, towards the approaching army. Cannon were discharged by the latter; but the balls went far over the heads of the imperial procession. Nearer and nearer they came; and, when within hearing, the native preachers accompanying the Emperor, and the Christian members of his guard, sang together an exultant Christian hymn. Almost paralyzed with astonishment, the rebels still slowly advanced. As they came within a few hundred yards, the Emperor[Pg 59] left his palanquin, and he and all his suite prostrated themselves in silent prayer to God. As if struck by a power from on high, the rebel soldiers, rank by rank, fell also to the ground; leaving their three chief leaders sitting on their horses alone. Then the Emperor and chief mandarin arose, and the latter solemnly bade the officers to do obeisance to their Emperor. One after another, they slowly dismounted, and each, as he came towards the Emperor, kneeled down, and, drawing his sword, performed the hara-kari, or national penal suicide. The chief mandarin, in a loud voice, commanded the people to return in peace to their homes, with the forgiveness and blessing of their Emperor. They obeyed; and the rebellion was at an end.

Of items of religious information nearer home, I may take note, that the Foreign Missionary Association of Philadelphia Yearly Meeting of Orthodox Friends has now seven missionaries in different fields; most of them engaged in Central Africa. The Society of Friends has altogether more than sixty foreign missionaries laboring in different parts of the world.

[Pg 60]

The missionaries sent out by all Protestant denominations together, from Europe and America, are hardly more numerous now than they were fifty years ago; their work being so much better done, generally, by their converts, the *native preachers*. Not an island in the Pacific is without its Christian church; not a spoken dialect in the world without its Bible. Yet the world has not, by any means, become altogether Christian, even in Christendom itself.

A great revival has just begun in Brooklyn. It has already reached New York, and is beginning to arouse interest in Philadelphia, Boston, and Baltimore. Crowds of men and women of all classes, especially the poorest and least cultivated, gather noon and night to religious services of a simple but most fervent character. Old men say they have known nothing like it since the days of 1857, or the Moody and Sankey meetings of 1874-76. By cable we learn that something of the same wave of religious movement has appeared in London, Berlin, and Paris. We ask, what are we to think of it? Is there a spiritual atmosphere, with its heights and depths, mysteriously swayed from land to land? We can only wait and see.

[Pg 61]
December 31st, 1931.

I have been reading over the pages of this diary for the year just coming to a close. This has led me to some retrospection, looking yet farther back, and comparing the present with the last century. The 19th century was proud of itself; and we of the 20th have hardly gained all that we should in true humility. Both centuries have had their great events and great advances; and both, their weaknesses, errors, and absurdities. I will venture a comparison of some of these.

The *most absurd* things of the 19th century, I think, were these: the decree at Rome of the infallibility of the Pope; England's bolstering up the Turkish Empire for fear of Russia attacking India; Lord Beaconsfield's administration altogether; the financial policy of the American green-back party; the belief in spirit-rapping, in the first principles of Herbert Spencer's philosophy, and in the sufficiency of Darwin's theory of natural selection to account for the ascent from lower to higher species; the shot-gun quarantine in the[Pg 62] South against yellow fever; the toleration of the waltz, in *otherwise civilized* society, when even Lord Byron denounced it; and the unreformed spelling of the English language.

As the greatest national *crimes* of the last century, I would name the British government forcing by war the trade in Opium upon China, and the long-continued bad faith of the United States government towards the Indian tribes of the West.

Perhaps the greatest *wonders* of the 19th century were the invention of photography, solar spectral analysis, the radiometer, the phonograph, the photophone; in public affairs, the reunion of the old and new school

22

Presbyterian Churches, and the disappearance, by civil war, of negro slavery in the United States.

The greatest *triumphs* of the first part of the 20th century have been the abandonment of all tariffs for protection in the United States, as well as in Europe, establishing perfectly free trade throughout the world; the successful introduction of woman's suffrage in almost every State of our Union; the acceptance of the principle of arbitration, through international congresses, in all[Pg 63]governmental disputes, by the great powers of both hemispheres; the practical conquest of intemperance, by the abolition of drinking-houses everywhere; and the disappearance of sectarianism amongst Christian denominations,—excepting only the persistently exclusive claims of the three great historical churches.

We are clearly not yet at the close of history. Is the world nearly prepared for its great consummation? Not yet are fulfilled the beautiful prophetic words of the poet Cowper, now far too seldom read:—

"Error has no place;
The creeping pestilence is driven away!
The breath of Heaven has chased it. In the heart
No passion touches a discordant string,
But all is harmony and love. Disease
Is not: the pure and uncontaminate blood
Holds its due course, nor fears the frost of age.
One song employs all nations; and all cry
'Worthy the Lamb, for he was slain for us!'
The dwellers in the vales and on the rocks
Shout to each other, and the mountain tops
From distant mountains catch the flying joy,—
Till, nation after nation taught the strain,
Earth rolls the rapturous hosanna round."

[Pg 64]

Not in our time have dawned such days as these. But, let our hearts be lifted up: *they will come yet.* Some New Year's bells will

"Ring out old shapes of foul disease;
Ring out the narrowing lust of gold;
Ring out the thousand wars of old,
Ring in the thousand years of peace.

Ring in the valiant man and free,
The larger heart, the kindlier hand;
Ring out the darkness of the land,
Ring in the Christ that is to be."